AF228589

HIKING

By Donna B. McKinney

SportsZone

An Imprint of Abdo Publishing
abdobooks.com

abdobooks.com

Published by Abdo Publishing, a division of ABDO, PO Box 398166, Minneapolis, Minnesota 55439. Copyright © 2020 by Abdo Consulting Group, Inc. International copyrights reserved in all countries. No part of this book may be reproduced in any form without written permission from the publisher. SportsZone™ is a trademark and logo of Abdo Publishing.

Printed in China
082019
012020

Cover Photo: Dudarev Mikhail/Shutterstock Images
Interior Photos: Monkey Business Images/Shutterstock Images, 5; Red Line Editorial, 7; Kurt Wilson/The Missoulian/AP Images, 8–9; Shutterstock Images, 11, 13, 37 (left), 37 (center), 42; iStockphoto, 14, 17, 21, 26; VM Jones/iStockphoto, 18; Joshua Resnick/Shutterstock Images, 22; Adventure Photo/iStockphoto, 25; Robert Mutch/Shutterstock Images, 29; Rawpixel.com/Shutterstock Images, 30; Les Palenik/Shutterstock Images, 33; Kichigin/Shutterstock Images, 35; Steven R. Smith/Shutterstock Images, 37 (right); Constance Joy/Shutterstock Images, 39; Larry Barrett/Shutterstock Images, 41; Casarsa Guru/iStockphoto, 45

Editor: Patrick Donnelly
Series Designer: Colleen McLaren

Library of Congress Control Number: 2019941984

Publisher's Cataloging-in-Publication Data

Names: McKinney, Donna B., author
Title: Hiking / by Donna B. McKinney
Description: Minneapolis, Minnesota : Abdo Publishing, 2020 | Series: Outdoor adventures | Includes online resources and index
Identifiers: ISBN 9781532190490 (lib. bdg.) | ISBN 9781532176340 (ebook)
Subjects: LCSH: Hiking--Juvenile literature. | Trekking--Juvenile literature. | Tramping--Juvenile literature. | Trails--Juvenile literature. | Outdoor recreation--Juvenile literature.
Classification: DDC 796.50--dc23

TABLE OF **CONTENTS**

LET'S GO HIKING

Reed Gjonnes started hiking with her dad when she was just four years old. Reed's dad is a skilled long-distance hiker. So at the start, hiking was just family fun for Reed.

"Hiking has been part of my life for as long as I can remember," Reed said in 2013, when she was in eighth grade. "When I was a little kid, it was because I wanted to spend time with my dad and go camping. Now I love everything about it—the beautiful scenery, the wild animals, and meeting other people on the trail. It's all pretty great."

Reed began looking for longer, more challenging hikes. She asked her dad if they could hike the Pacific Crest Trail. It runs a length of 2,650 miles (4,265 km),

Trail hiking is fun for people of all ages.

4

stretching from Mexico to Canada. That was just the start of a big adventure.

Before she turned 14, Reed and her dad had hiked the three longest trails in the United States. She hiked the Pacific Crest Trail at age 11. Next, she hiked the 2,192 miles (3,528 km) of the Appalachian Trail at age 12. And at age 13, she hiked the Continental Divide Trail, which covers 3,100 miles (4,989 km). Hiking all of these three trails is called the "Triple Crown" of hiking. Through 2018, only approximately 400 people had achieved the Triple Crown. And Reed was the youngest person known to have hiked all three trails. The Triple Crown totals 7,942 miles (12,781 km). To complete the Triple Crown with her dad, Reed hiked in 22 states and wore out six pairs of shoes.

Reed's hikes are amazing. But a new hiker can learn the basics, starting with short, simple day hikes. As hikers gain skill, they can tackle longer trails. Hiking is a sport in which age and athletic ability do not matter so much. Hikers can choose trails ranging from a flat path through the woods to mountain climbing.

—TRIPLE CROWN HIKES—

People can choose a hike that suits their ability and build from there to more difficult hikes.

HEALTHY ACTIVITY FOR YOUNG AND OLD

Hiking is both fun and good for a person. With hiking comes the fun of being outdoors and enjoying the

scenery. But there are many health benefits with hiking too. Hiking helps improve cardiovascular health while strengthening hip and leg muscles. The core muscles around the middle of the body are strengthened by hiking too. A person's balance is

improved by hiking. And hiking is good for the mind,
helping to boost a person's mood and ease stress.

Some people enjoy solo hiking. But it is more fun,
and safer, to hike with others. That makes hiking
a great activity for family members and friends to

COLLECT PARK PASSPORT STAMPS

Hikers who visit the many state and national parks across the United States can collect passport stamps. These stamps are a fun way to keep track of the hikes they have taken. Hikers can get a park passport book at most parks. When hikers visit a new park, a park employee will place a stamp in their books.

do together. And because athletic ability is not as important as in some other sports, people of different ages can enjoy hiking together.

For some sports, people need to buy a lot of costly gear just to get started. But for hiking, a person can begin with just a sturdy pair of sneakers and some comfortable clothes. Hikers can always add other gear later. But a lack of hiking gear should not stop a person from just going on a hike right now. So lace up a pair of sneakers and hit the trails!

It doesn't require a lot of fancy gear to go on a hike.

CHAPTER 2

WHAT TO WEAR

Some sports require a special kind of clothing or uniform, but not hiking. Many hikers already have most of the clothes needed for hiking.

Some hikers recommend dressing like an onion. When an onion is peeled, it reveals multiple, thin layers underneath. So dressing like an onion means wearing thin layers of clothes. Those thin layers help keep a hiker comfortable in warm or cool weather. The layers dry quickly when a hiker gets damp from rain or sweat. And with thin layers of clothes, a hiker can add or remove layers as needed as temperatures rise or fall.

Hikers usually wear long pants or heavy tights to keep their legs from getting scratched in the woods.

Hiking at high altitudes requires warm clothing.

Also, jeans or heavy cotton clothes are not the best choice for hiking. These clothes are very uncomfortable if they get wet. They hold the moisture close to the skin.

Many hikers prefer wool clothes. Wool and wool blends have the reputation of being scratchy, but they also can be soft. They do a great job of holding in body heat, even when the fabric gets wet. Another option for hikers is workout gear. Clothing made for sports or active wear is usually moisture wicking. It does a good job of allowing moisture to evaporate off of skin.

Hikers should wear long pants if they want to avoid getting their legs scratched.

Fleece provides warmth and protection from the wind. Long sleeves that roll up are a good choice. They protect hikers from cool temperatures and sunburn. A hat keeps a hiker's head warm. Hats with brims, such as a baseball cap or a wide-brimmed hat, also provide good sun protection.

STEP SMARTLY

The average person takes approximately 2,000 steps to walk one mile (1.6 km). So a hiker's shoes or boots and socks are important. Sneakers or trail-running shoes work well. Hiking more difficult, longer, or wet trails might require hiking boots or hiking shoes. These give better support for the ankles and feet. Shoes or boots need to fit well so they do not rub against the feet and cause blisters. Hikers' shoes should keep their feet dry and provide a good grip for walking the trail. And they should be lightweight. Hiking gives the legs and feet enough of a workout. There is no need to add a heavy pair of shoes into the mix.

Socks that are wool, wool blend, or synthetic are best for hiking. They help keep a hiker's feet dry, which helps prevent blisters. Cotton socks hold moisture close to the feet. This can lead to rubbing and blisters.

PASS THE SUNSCREEN

Any skin that is exposed to the sun can get sunburned, regardless of the air temperature. So even in cooler weather, it is smart to wear sunscreen. Sunglasses are also handy for hikers. They protect the eyes and make it easier to see where to step in bright sunshine.

Weather can change quickly. A day that starts out warm can change if temperatures drop or rain starts. Also, temperatures in the woods are cooler than out in the sunshine. Smart hikers are prepared for weather changes. Hikers should bring a waterproof jacket and an extra lightweight layer of clothes, just in case the weather brings surprises.

Hikers need to be prepared for all types of weather.

CHAPTER 3

WHAT TO PACK

Water is among the first concerns when determining a packing list. Just as it does when competing in other sports, the body needs plenty of water while hiking. As a person hikes, the body gets warmer. It gets rid of the excess heat by sweating. When the sweat evaporates, the body cools. Hikers need to replace that lost fluid or they risk dehydration. Dehydration occurs when people do not drink enough water. It can make them sick. And while soft drinks and other beverages might taste refreshing, they do not give the body the water it needs.

The American College of Sports Medicine says to drink at least 16 to 20 ounces (500 to 600 ml) of water one to two hours before an outdoor activity

There's a lot to think about when deciding what to pack for a hike.

like hiking. While hiking, drink six to 12 ounces
(180 to 360 ml) of water every 10 to 15 minutes. After
hiking, hikers should drink another 16 to 24 ounces
(500 to 800 ml) to replenish the body.

For most short day hikes, plenty of water and some
healthy snacks are all a hiker needs. For longer hikes
or overnight camping, meals are needed, too. This
means choosing foods that are easy to carry and
prepare and packing plates and cooking utensils.
Hikers need to be able to prepare and cook food and
then clean up. All this means that hikers need to do
some smart meal planning before heading into the
woods for longer trips.

OUCH! BRING THE FIRST AID KIT

Scrapes, cuts, bug bites, and blisters can be a real
bummer on the trail. Sometimes hikers need a first
aid kit. The kit doesn't have to be large. Some hikers
put together their own basic kits. Sporting goods
stores also sell prepackaged kits.

It's important to drink plenty of water before, during, and after a hike.

Hikers should carry safety gear in case something goes wrong on the hike. A whistle lets hikers call for help if they're hurt or lost. And a whistle can help hikers who get separated find each other. The sound of a whistle carries farther than a person's voice. Matches or a lighter helps a hiker start a fire, if needed. A headlamp or flashlight is handy, especially if a hiker will be in the woods as it starts to get dark. An emergency blanket also helps in case the weather suddenly turns cold or wet.

Many hikers carry a knife. It can be a simple, single-blade pocket knife. Some prefer more complex knives with tools such as a screwdriver, bottle opener, can opener, or scissors attached.

CARRYING THE LOAD

A backpack allows hikers to easily carry the supplies they need. When people first start to hike, any backpack they have could work. But people who plan to continue hiking would benefit from a backpack

A headlamp can help light the way after the sun goes down.

Most granola bars are filled with the nutrients hikers need on the trail.

made for hiking. Hikers should shop for a backpack that fits them just right—not too large and not too small. Backpacks come in sizes to fit children, women, and men. Day packs are meant for short hikes. Bigger packs are available for longer hikes or overnight camping.

Hikers should pack wisely to avoid having to carry too much weight. For a day hike, the heaviest items in the backpack should be water and food. For short hikes, other items might be sunglasses, sunscreen, bug spray, a whistle, a pocket knife, a trash bag, a rain jacket, and a simple first aid kit.

Some backpacks are hydration backpacks. This means they carry the hiker's water supply in a container that fits snugly inside the pack. This container is called a reservoir or bladder. It's attached to a long, flexible straw that lets the hiker easily drink the water without stopping to reach inside the pack. These packs are very useful in hot summer weather.

CHAPTER 4

WHERE TO GO

For a new hiker just starting out, there are safe, easy ways to learn about hiking. Hikers can start at the local parks in their area. Regular visits to hike at local parks help new hikers in several ways.

For instance, hikers can test out their gear. Is the backpack a good fit? Are they carrying too much heavy gear? Do their hiking boots create blisters? Hiking familiar local parks allows hikers to gain strength and skill in the woods.

When planning hikes beyond local parks, a hiker should consider several questions. Is the hiker experienced or new to hiking? Is the hiker physically strong? What is the terrain like—flat and easy to hike, or rocky and rough? Is it in the mountains?

Local parks can provide plenty of convenient trails for beginning hikers.

A good map can help hikers find their way.

Thinking about these kinds of questions helps a hiker decide what kind of hike to do and where to go.

FIND A HIKING CLUB

A new hiker might also want to look for any local hiking clubs or groups. For the beginning hiker, a club can be a good place to meet more experienced hikers. Hikers can make new friends and learn new skills in these groups.

There are plenty of books about hiking. The public library or a local bookstore could be a good place to find these books. A web search for "hiking" or "hiking in (your state name)" should yield lots of information, too.

Some outfitter stores offer hiking or backpacking classes. Do a web search for "hiking classes near me" to find what might be offered. These classes can be a great way to learn from more experienced hikers before heading off to the woods.

THE HIKING PROJECT

The Hiking Project is a website and a mobile app with information about hiking trails. It features maps and other information about trails across the United States and in other countries, too. Trails are listed state by state for the United States. Altogether it has information on more than 58,000 trails.

The Hiking Project helps hikers plan trips and share information about hiking. Its website—hikingproject.com—is always changing as hikers add new information.

For hikes in state or national parks, the park office can provide trail maps. In these parks, trails are usually marked with colors called "blazes." These blazes are painted on or attached to trees or posts to show the trail. The well-marked trails are helpful for hikers of all ages and experience levels. But for the new hiker, these marked trails are a safe and effective way to learn good hiking skills.

The place where a hiking trail begins is called the trailhead. Sometimes a

Colorful blazes help hikers stay on the trail.

signboard with maps or other helpful information will greet hikers at the trailhead.

Because it can be easy to get turned around in the woods, it is smart for a hiker to learn basic navigation skills. Hikers sometimes use a map, a compass, or a handheld Global Positioning System (GPS) tracker to help them navigate.

DO YOUR HOMEWORK

To be safe and have fun, smart hikers plan before going on a hike. Here are some questions they might think about.

WHAT IS THE WEATHER FORECAST?

Sunny skies at the moment do not mean sunshine all day. Hikers should check the weather forecast before leaving home. Knowing the forecast helps a hiker choose the right clothes. In some cases, knowing the forecast might help a hiker decide to wait for better weather. Hikers should always be listening and

Checking the weather forecast can help a hiker decide how to dress or even whether to go out that day.

watching for thunderstorms. The safest place during a thunderstorm is indoors.

ARE ANY TRAILS CLOSED?

When hiking at any of the state or national parks, it is smart to check with the park ranger or park office before heading into the woods. Some trails could be closed, especially if there has been too much rain or flooding recently.

IS THAT POISON IVY?

Hikers need to be alert for poisonous plants and wildlife. Poison ivy has a familiar three-leaf pattern. Poison oak and poison sumac often have more leaves. Hikers need to know what these plants look like so they can stay away from them.

Hikers should also watch for stinging nettles. These plants can cause a painful burning sensation for those who touch them. There can also be wild berries in the woods that look good to eat. Hikers should not eat them. The berries provide food for

—WATCH YOUR STEP!—

Keep an eye out for these poisonous plants if you want to avoid an itchy aftermath to your hike.

Poison Oak **Poison Sumac** **Poison Ivy**

animals, and some of those berries are poisonous to humans. The best choice for hikers is to just eat the snacks in their backpacks.

Ticks are common across much of the United States. They are especially problematic during the warm summer months. Ticks can carry diseases. So can mosquitoes. Hikers should use a bug spray that protects against ticks, mosquitoes, and black flies. After a hike, people should carefully check their clothes, scan their bodies, and search their heads

WHAT IS GEOCACHING?

Some hikers enjoy geocaching. It's like a treasure hunt in nature. Hikers use a handheld GPS device to track and find objects hidden by other geocachers. The object is usually a waterproof container with a logbook to sign and date. To get started, hikers can get a free online account at geocaching.com.

for ticks. It is wise to bathe or shower within two hours of hiking to wash away any ticks before they can bite.

ARE THERE SNAKES?

Hikers who spend a lot of time in the woods have a good chance of seeing a snake. Most snakes avoid people. But if stepped on or surprised, snakes can bite. There are many kinds of snakes. They vary in size, color, and markings.

Most poisonous snakes have broad, wedge-shaped heads. Nonpoisonous snakes have heads shaped like a triangle, but somewhat rounded. Poisonous snakes have eyes with vertical slits. Nonpoisonous snakes have round eyes. Poisonous snakes tend to be bigger and fatter than nonpoisonous ones. Do not depend on hearing a rattle sound to know if a snake is poisonous. Rattlesnakes are not the only poisonous

snakes in the United States. Some do not make a sound. The best thing a hiker can do when seeing a snake is to freeze and then step away from the snake, moving slowly backward.

WHO KNOWS WHERE I AM GOING?

Hikers should always be sure to tell someone where they are going and a general time to expect their return. This includes the starting point—where they plan to enter the woods. Hiking with a buddy is the smart way to travel. A hike is usually more fun traveling with a buddy. And if there is an accident, buddies can help each other.

KEEP IT CLEAN

Some sports have lots of rules for players to follow. Hiking does not have rules like some sporting events. But among hikers, there are some good manners that people are expected to follow. These can be summed up quite simply: respect other hikers and respect the wilderness.

RESPECT ALL THE WILDLIFE

Hikers leave animals alone. This means not feeding the animals. Giving animals human food might keep them from doing a good job of hunting for food for themselves.

Some parks allow dogs on leashes. Hikers who want to hike with their dogs should check with the park office first to be sure it is allowed. To help keep

Dogs should stay leashed during a hike.

the dog and the wildlife safe, the dog must be on a leash at all times while hiking.

BE POLITE ON THE HIKE

These rules for polite behavior usually are not posted on the hiking trail. But experienced hikers know to follow them. Hiking is a quiet activity. No loud talking or loud music on the trail. Hikers should turn their cell phones down or off. If hikers want to listen to music, they should wear headphones or earbuds.

Hikers who pause to rest should step to the side of the trail to let other hikers pass. When hiking with a group, hikers should not block the whole trail. Instead, they should walk in a way that allows other hikers to pass. When meeting another hiker on the trail, it is polite to nod or say hello.

Rules for right-of-way on hiking trails make hiking safer for everyone. Hikers moving downhill give space to let hikers going uphill pass through. Bikers yield and let hikers and horseback riders pass through. Hikers must yield to horseback riders.

NATIONAL TRAILS DAY

The first Saturday in June is National Trails Day. The American Hiking Society sponsors the day. Across the United States, special events encourage people to get out and hike. The American Hiking Society provides details about National Trails Day events and other helpful information at americanhiking.org.

LEAVE NO TRACE

The American Hiking Society says, "Leave what you find—take only photos and memories." There are many ways for hikers to leave no trace when they go into the woods. For starters, they can enjoy witnessing the beauty of nature without taking anything—a leaf, a rock, a flower—home with them.

If a campfire is needed, hikers should keep it very small. They should find and use constructed fire rings or fire mounds. They should not let the fire damage any live or fallen trees. Small camping stoves usually work much better than campfires for cooking.

Hikers should stay on the trail when hiking. Taking shortcuts means disturbing the wilderness. The trails are there for a good reason, and smart hikers follow the trails.

Another way for hikers to leave no trace when they hike is to carry a trash bag. Hikers should carry every piece of trash—even the smallest thing—out in their

Some trails offer receptacles for trash and recyclables; otherwise, hikers must carry every bit of trash with them.

trash bags. As time passes, trash left behind can have a big impact on the wilderness.

Hiking can be a lifelong sport. People of all ages enjoy it. The benefits of hiking are many. So gather your gear, call a hiking buddy, and head to the woods.

GLOSSARY

blazes
Colorful markers that show hikers the hiking trail.

dehydration
A significant loss of body fluid that impairs normal body functions.

geocaching
A game similar to a treasure hunt in which people find hidden items using a GPS device.

GPS
The Global Positioning System that uses satellite signals to allow people to determine locations.

moisture wicking
Pulling moisture away from a person's skin, cooling the person as the moisture evaporates.

national parks
Areas across the United States protected by the federal government, allowing people to enjoy the lands and the wildlife within them.

passport stamp
An ink stamp or sticker hikers can get as they visit each of the national or state parks.

state parks
Recreation areas located in every state in the United States.

terrain
The physical features of a stretch of land.

ticks
Tiny bugs that can spread disease when they bite humans.

trailhead
The place where a hiking trail begins.

MORE INFORMATION

BOOKS

Hengel, Katherine. *Cool Parks & Trails: Great Things to Do in the Great Outdoors*. Minneapolis, MN: Abdo, 2016.

Olsson, Helen. *Ranger Rick Kids' Guide to Hiking: All You Need to Know about Having Fun While Hiking*. Mission Viejo, CA: Walter Foster, 2018.

Skurka, Andrew. *The Ultimate Hiker's Gear Guide: Tools and Techniques to Hit the Trail*. Washington, DC: National Geographic, 2017.

ONLINE RESOURCES

To learn more about hiking, please visit **abdobooklinks.com** or scan this QR code. These links are routinely monitored and updated to provide the most current information available.

INDEX

ABOUT THE AUTHOR

Donna B. McKinney is a writer who lives in North Carolina. She spent many years writing about science and technology topics at the US Naval Research Laboratory in Washington, DC. Now she enjoys writing about topics including science, history, and sports for children and young adults. Her goal is to hike all 40 state parks in North Carolina—so far she has completed hikes at 15 of them.